Massage Marketing

Don't Leave Money on

The Table

Earn More Money with An Infusion Of Creative Services

To Reel In More Clients

Sabrina Tonneson

For permissions contact: SabrinaTonneson@gmail.com

ISBN: 978-1-947125-04-9

Author's website www.MassageMarketing101.om

Dedicated to Moriah and Andre'

Table of Contents

Introduction

So you've just delivered one of your signature, stress-obliterating massages. The client gushes about your magic fingers as they leave the table. There goes another satisfied customer.

Yet, as you pack away the massage paraphernalia, you're left with a niggling feeling something isn't quite right. Your massage therapy practice isn't garnering the same satisfaction your clients walk away with. Stuck in a financial rut, the profits your hands work so hard to earn aren't materializing.

Well, the good news is all of that is going to change! With the application of the remedies detailed in this book, you'll start to see a turnaround in your business fortunes with some solid, money-spinning strategies!

You've got the talent and work ethic, no doubt. A critical component for a wildly successful massage therapy practice, though, is taking the leap beyond the basic flat rate massage.

Sticking with a basic flat rate massage is the surest path to flat lining business growth. Creating a services menu can be one of your most effective massage marketing tools. You need to grasp the power of options and the importance of reaching out to a variety of customers with irresistible packages. The key to attracting better profits is tailor-made offerings for different client demographics.

Many massage therapists funnel all their energies into their craft, but need help conceptualizing ideas to create a menu. The profit-boosting principles explored in this book allow anyone in the massage therapy business to transform the performance of their practice.

This book, Massage Marketing: Don't Leave Money on the Table is the follow up to Massage Marketing: Boost Profits, Earn More, Work Less By Implementing a Strategic Pricing Menu.

It demonstrates why a menu and creative packaging are key stepping stones to financial success. While some folks are on board with the idea of creating a business menu, imagining what services they can offer is where they get stuck. Well, have no fear! I'm here to teach you how to create and showcase packages in an appealing way.

My name is Sabrina Tonneson and I have over two decades of massage therapy experience. From head to toe, I'll give you ideas to make every inch of skin your fingers travel count. You'll learn how to conceive wonderfully decadent packages to lure clients on both tight and open budgets. It's time to turn your business into a real money making proposition!

Grow Your Business Quickly

That's what we all want, a business that shows robust growth with healthy profits. One of the best ways to germinate that growth is with the development of a spa package to accommodate a variety of services. Don't limit your scope for expansion by obsessing about your budget or room size.

Tech titan and Apple co-founder Steve Jobs' vision was born in a garage, so you shouldn't allow your current circumstances to dictate your future successes. The most important thing is getting to work on your vision with packages that fit a range of budgets. That is a sure-fire path to kick starting your healthy income breakthrough.

Temporary offers are a smart marketer's secret. Test out an idea with a temporary offer. The test is not only for feedback from clients but also from the massage therapists. One business I consulted wanted to introduce the popular sugar scrubs. The business invested in the sugar scrub product and started to promote. Customers enjoyed it, but the therapists did not! All the therapists complained the sugar scrub was challenging to remove. Even after they washed their hands, the sugar crystals somehow seemed everywhere. If a product is hard to remove or clean, it can create challenges for the rest of the treatment. The business tried a foot masque instead of sugar scrub and the therapists were happy.

Customers liked both. If your team of therapists are unhappy with a product, it is not a win win. Luckily the business did not print materials with sugar scrub and they were easily able to modify the offer to design a win win package.

Another benefit of a temporary offer is to determine how much product you use. If a treatment is taking more product than you expected, the profits might not be large enough for the package to be an asset. If the price of package is too high, and customers are not buying the package, the products can get old and expire.

Temporary offers allow you to tweak your package. You can experience through trial and error not only what you want to include in the package, but how much you want to charge for the package.

#1 Tip for Success

Become a customer. Imagine yourself as a massage therapy customer. Stay with me here. One of the best things you can do to get repeat clients is to become a regular massage customer yourself!

If you don't have a lot of folding money lying around for monthly massages, you can trade them. Trading massages, though, isn't the same as being a regular paying customer. When the money leaves your pocket after an hour of service, your expectations of what constitutes a good massage experience change.

My sage advice to all massage therapists is get a massage every month by someone new. When you sample new businesses and new therapists, you become connected to the service and what your customers feel. It's a toss of the dice, you can't be sure if you'll love or hate the experience. Trying out different therapists expands your exposure to a variety of techniques. Some techniques will sizzle while others fizzle. You need to go out there and find out which is which.

One therapist whom I had coached admitted, after a lengthy interrogation under hot lights, that she did not get regular massages. After some prodding, she resolved to get one or two massages per month.

Well, this therapist returned to me with glowing reports that her business increased. As the therapist become the massaged, she felt a shift. She confessed she had been feeling like a hypocrite advising her clients to make regular visits, while she herself often waited several months between massages.

Once she started getting regular massages, though, and began to absorb all of the benefits, this gave her practice an added authenticity.

Another welcome result of her massage excursions was a noticeable increase in tips! It suddenly dawned on her that when she took the time to keep her own mind and body in balance, she had more to offer to her clients. This, in turn, enabled her to extract greater enjoyment from her practice. Thus began a happy deluge of compliments, tips and that golden ticket; referrals!

Now, this next story will sound strange, but bear with me. One experience that really shaped my business and helped me quickly multiply repeat clients was receiving an awful massage. That's not to say you should go in search of a massage therapist who will knead your back like dough, but here goes: I rolled out of bed one morning with a sore, tight neck. I needed massage therapy! There was a place charging more than I was wanted to part with, but it was the only business with an opening.

During my consultation with the therapist, I advised that she dedicate the entire session to my neck and back. Peculiarly, she had other ideas and kept trying to pressure me into a full body massage. I sensed she was a bit of a novice and didn't know how to give a neck and back massage only. I finally let her talk me into doing my arms because she was mule-stubborn about what she wanted to do.

The massage was average, but the whole time she was doing my arms I was annoyed. I didn't want my arms done. My fingers weren't a priority at that moment. My neck was in pain, and now my massage therapist was another pain in my neck. It doesn't take an expert to know that if your massage therapist leaves you feeling irritable, that's the exact opposite of what you'd expect from a session.

That dreadful experience really helped me appreciate the customer's point of view. Give your clients what they ask for.

But wait, there's more! During yet another memorably disappointing session, I had requested extra work on my hamstrings and quadriceps. A punishing stair machine workout left my legs quite sore. The therapist was skilled enough and gave a great massage.

There was one exception, though, she spent one or two minutes on each leg. If someone asks for extra work on two muscle groups and you have 90 minutes, how much time would you spend on those muscle groups? Yes, it does sound like a math quiz question, but I was so irritated. One of two things happened, she either ignored my request or didn't care. Either way, I lost out! Just recounting those incidents gives me hankering for a massage...from a therapist who listens!

Those unpleasant experiences really helped me grow my customer base quickly. They taught me that knowing what not to do is as important as knowing what you should do. There is no doubt that in massage school my massage tormentors were taught to be attentive to their customers. People often fail to learn these important lessons until they experience the frustration first hand. When it comes to squandering someone's time and money, it gets personal.

To this very day, I try to get a weekly massage, auditioning a new business every month. Chiropractors, fitness centers, day spas and massage centers; I try them all with an open mind. This wealth of experience allowed me to rapidly grow my business. I can't put too fine a point on this: being a consumer of the service you sell is the best advice I have for any massage therapist.

Create the Ambiance - Lighting

So building up massage experiences to influence the quality of your own massage therapy practice is key. Just as important, though, is the environment you create for your clients.

Remember, a massage is supposed to be a relaxing experience, a manipulation of the muscles to chisel away tension in the body and mind. If the lighting in your massage therapy room can compete with a stadium on Super Bowl night, here's a hint: take it down a notch.

Bright lighting makes relaxation challenging. With a dimming switcher, you can control the lamps and lighting in your massage therapy to create an environment conducive to relaxation and blissful repose. Dimmer switches are affordable and easy to use.

Create The Ambiance - Eye Pillow

Here is another exceptional value add-on to your practice: give eye pillows ago. A massage with an eye pillow is a low cost extra that can help your clients drift off into an ethereal state of dreaminess. Never heard of it? You don't know what you're missing. It's almost like being drugged, except you won't wake up in an abandoned warehouse surrounded by swinging meat hooks.

Amazon has a variety of eye pillows to choose from. Here's a useful tip, heat your eye pillow. After you've finished the face and neck massage, place the warm eye pillow on your client's eyes. If you haven't tried this before, incorporate it into your next massage. Your customer will really go for them.

The darkness helps quiet frenetic minds and allows your clients to sink into a deep state of relaxation. Place a fresh Kleenex under the eye pillow for each client.

Create The Ambiance - Scents

Massage therapy is, in many ways, the seductive art of stimulating the senses. While you work primarily with the sense of touch, smell is another pathway to euphoric serenity. That's why you should use the gift of smell to create a warm, welcoming atmosphere.

There are many techniques to employ scents in your massage therapy practice. Spa diffusers are invaluable tools in optimizing your clients' sense of smell. Again, Amazon is a great marketplace to find diffusers of varying sizes and costs. You may want to buy a few diffusers depending on the size of your business and rooms.

At the beginning of the day, you can select the scent you want and drop essential oils into the diffuser's water reservoir. You should use the same oils in all of your diffusers to create one uniform, pleasant odor throughout your business. Too much mixing and you might end up with a potpourri atmosphere. Some therapists go for a stronger bouquet, others like something understated.

Candles are another great way to perfume your business. You can light enough candles to create the right mood and scent, but not so many that it looks like a séance. It's important to observe all fire prevention protocols and make sure you have a functioning fire extinguisher if you intend to use scented candles.

The possibilities for experimenting with scents are really limitless. If you have a crockpot with hot towels, try placing a few drops of essential oils on your wet towels. When you open the lid to get a hot towel, the pleasing odors will billow out.

I like to swing the hot scented towel near to the client's head. The smell of peppermint permeates the room and the client's senses. It can even clear blocked sinuses.

Aromatherapy and massages have been at the heart of some truly amazing experiences. In fact, my memory has preserved one such experience in California. The massage in question was approaching the end. I was lying face down when, suddenly, the unmistakable scent of peppermint found my nose. It wasn't there during the massage, but it suddenly materialized, announcing itself like the first day of spring!

It was refreshing and welcoming. When the treatment ended and I was getting dressed, I went into detective mode. I snooped around to see if I could spot the diffuser from whence this intoxicating aroma had issued. There was nothing to be found. Never one to be shy, I asked the therapist how she got her scents game so strong. She revealed her mystery technique; using just a few drops of essential oils in her palms, she deftly waved them beneath the face cradle. In waving her hands, the peppermint aroma pervaded the atmosphere. It was mind-blowing how such a simple technique could create a valuable add-on to a massage therapy practice.

Imitation is the sincerest form of flattery and I adopted that modest, yet powerful technique of building an aroma-filled environment for my clients. My efforts didn't go unnoticed, commendations from customers flowed in abundance. This technique is particularly useful because some clients' sinuses become congested when they lie face down. The peppermint trick relieves the blockage, and the clients absolutely love it.

Create The Ambiance - Layout and Design

There is one final point of discussion when it comes to making your business warm and welcoming. You may be familiar with the phrase, "You never get a second chance to make a first impression."

Ask yourself, what's the first impression you want your customers to have when they walk into your practice? If increased profit and repeat business is your sort of thing, you want to be sure that your clients are exposed to the most appealing design and layout you can muster.

Neat and tidy is the first place to start. If your practice appears cluttered and you look disheveled, a client is liable to extrapolate that first impression to the quality of service you offer. If you're finding items in your office which cannot justify their presence there, they should be discarded. When clients walk into your practice, they should immediately feel as though they have stepped off the streets and onto a cloud.

As you may not be the best judge of your business's character, invite some friends over and have them give you their unvarnished impressions of your space.

If you're thinking about a business an upgrade, a simple yet tasteful paint job could do the trick. You don't need to break the bank to create the most welcoming atmosphere.

Create The Ambiance - Massage Table

Here's an important question, how comfortable is your massage table? Think about it, your clients will be laid out on this table for between 60 and 90 minutes. A comfortable table can be a soothing centerpiece asset to your practice.

Invest a little thought and time into making your massage table a plush cradle of comfort, and watch as your clients literally deflate...ahhh...as they slip into a state of relaxation bordering on catatonic.

If you've ever been on a hard massage table, then you'd know it's pure torture. Indeed, one of my worst massage table experiences was on a cruise ship. The price was double precisely because it was a cruise ship so I was expecting decadent pampering on a massage table that should have made me feel I was being levitated by sorcery.

Instead, I was laid out on a narrow plank of a table that was as hard as a diamond. I've tried massages on three different cruise ships and the tables were all invariably awful. I might as well have been laid out on the street. I love a good massage as much as anyone else, but to be crucified on a rock-hard table for 75 minutes is too great a test of my faith.

So how do you create a great massage table on a budget? Head off to a Walmart or Target-type store and, in the bedding section, pick up some foam for a single or double bed. If you buy for a double bed, cut or fold the foam. Before putting on your sheets, lay out the foam. Next, you'll want to add some heat. For that, use a twin-size heating blanket.

Massage table heating blankets are usually twice the price, so if you use a twin-size you'll pay less. You can check out trusty old Amazon for some great deals. If you live in winter states, stores tend to offer their heating blankets on sale in the months of February and March. It's a good idea to pick up the sale item and keep an extra blanket in case one fails on you.

A twin-size mattress pad is also a good investment. The heat and the cushion from the foam will add that extra layer of dreamy comfort to your massage table.

If money's no object, then get the memory foam. It costs over $100.00, but good memory foam will give your clients a memorable experience. See what I did there?

I love to patronize massage businesses which use memory foam. When I get up on that table, I just drift off into a realm where all my troubles dissipate. Massage therapists usually have a hard time getting me off such a table!

Create The Ambiance - Neck Pillow

You should offer a pillow to elevate your customers' head after a neck, scalp and face massage. Lying flat on your back isn't the most comfortable sensation. Throw a pillow in there and the experience will be much more enjoyable for your clients.

You can use pillows as well as towels. Take a towel, roll it up, and place it beneath the neck. Some massage therapists purchase a hot towel caddy and store dry towels in them. They use a rolled up, heated, dry towel to place under the neck.

The Art Of Hot Towels

You can buy a crockpot at one of those big box or general stores and use it for your hot towels and hot stones. Here's how you do it: wet your hand towels and rinse them well. The more residual water in the towel, the hotter it will be. You can use hot towels in many ways; scalp treatments, face treatments, foot treatments and on the back.

One important thing to remember when working with hot towels is that they get cold quickly. Some massage therapists will wrap a foot in a hot towel, then go and massage the leg. By the time they return to the hot towel, it has cooled off. A cold wet towel on the skin is like having a large frog on your back. Don't ask me how I know that, just trust me, it is an unpleasant feeling.

In one unforgettable experience I had with a cold, soggy towel, my massage therapist started my session with a hot towel on my back. She was getting full points already. Ahh, it felt wonderful!

With the hot towel still on my back, she moved on to my legs. The towel cooled off and I started to feel cold. Ahhh, changed to ughh! I couldn't even enjoy the work she was doing on my legs as I could only think of this cold, wet towel/frog on my back. I finally had to ask, "could you please remove that cold, sorry towel from my back?"

Here's a neat trick to solving that problem. Put a heated towel on yourself and time how long it takes to cool down to the point of being uncomfortable. Then you will know first hand how quickly the towel cools.

There are two great tips for using hot towels on the back.

Tip 1) Place a dry towel on the back first, then lay your hot wet towels on top of the dry towel. Do your compressions on the towels. When you go remove the towels, the client's back will neither be wet nor will it have a cold sensation from the air as the towel is lifted off.

Tip 2) Lay a wet towel on the client's back, do your compressions, then pull up your sheet. After you've raised the sheet, remove the wet towel. The sheet will prevent the cold air from chilling your client's back after the towel has been removed.

Don't do compressions on top of sheet with the hot towel underneath, as the sheet will absorb moisture from the towel. A damp sheet is no fun either.

Hot towels are the most affordable way to enhance a package. Towels can be washed and re-used over and over again. You can be creative with towels. One customer had aching, sore forearms. I took a heated towel and wrapped it around her forearm and did compressions. She told me it was the best forearm massage she ever received.

Learning New Techniques

Massage therapists often create their signature massage. This is the massage by which customers come to know the therapist. There is a routine which becomes easy enough to perform on autopilot.

However, performing the same massage day in and day out can become quite tedious. One way to keep things fresh and to stay motivated is through the incorporation of new techniques.

One of the best open universities to learn new ideas is YouTube. Yes, YouTube is a fantastic resource, even beyond videos of precocious babies, mischievous cats and adorable baby cats. You can research any massage technique under the sun, with thousands of free videos available with instructional tips. If you want to learn how to include hot stones in your massage practice, you can simply search hot stone instruction videos.

Instructional DVDs are also widely available if you want to narrow your search for useful training materials, you can visit Massage Warehouse or even Amazon and investigate new modalities.

Workshops and CEU classes are also invaluable training resources.

I have discovered that therapists who set a goal of learning something new every month, feel more rejuvenated when they are working. They may or may not use a new technique they've picked up, but it gives them more options to pack into their box of tricks. Keeping an open mind and assimilating new techniques is a great way to keep the mind stimulated.

One therapist I coached decided to take a massage cupping course and was pleasantly surprised by how much she enjoyed it. Additionally, she was thrilled to see how this newly-acquired knowledge benefited her clients. This therapist offered clients a free sample of the service, and then developed it as an add- on to her range of services.

Now over 20% of her clients regularly request this upgrade. She even reeled in a few new clients because she is one of the few businesses in her area offering massages cupping. Picking up additional skills enabled this therapist to increase her profits while maintaining healthy stimulation of her mind.

Get Raving Fans With Hot Stones

Hot stones are a popular item in the massage business. The return on your investment will be over 1,000 fold. Customers absolutely love them. The stones are versatile as you can use full hot body stones or only concentrate the use of stones on certain muscle groups or focus areas.

A note of caution when working with hot stones, you will want to apply special care when working with the elderly. As we age, our skin becomes thinner and less resilient. If you are working with an elderly client, it's a good idea to go easy on the heat. You want to relax, not cook your client. I would recommend having your clients sign a release form in which they agree to communicate if the stones are too hot or are in any way a discomfort.

Hot stones are very flexible in their applications. Try out a massage using hot stones yourself so you can get an appreciation for the many ways they can be used.

There are cold stones, salt stones and Corestones, all of which can be used for different treatments. You can build different packages around these stones, thereby, adding to your diverse list of services.

Cold stones are effective in reducing inflammation while Corestones are great for sports massages. One of my preferred hot stone treatments is Corestones for facial massage. These uniquely designed stones allow you to deliver a soothing hot stone face massage that customers crave!

If you want to learn more about these hot stone options, you can Google them and watch them on YouTube, preferably before the baby, cat and baby cat videos.

Some people find their own stones in nature. Not all stones, though, are created equal. While some will be great for your massage therapy practice, others are better suited to construction or throwing through the windows of tiresome neighbors.

Before using your stones on customers, try them out on family and friends to double check whether they deliver the desired results. If after those experiments they still consider themselves your family and friends, you know you are good to go.

When it comes to heating the stones, the most effective tool I've ever used is a slow cooker. These can be bought at Walmart-type stores for a fraction of the cost of professional hot stone heaters. The benefit of a slow cooker is the temperature range. You can find the temperature that works for you and control the settings.

Crockpots with only warm, low and high settings can be problematic in achieving a consistent temperature. The main downside to a slow cooker is size. If you are working with a tight space, it can be tough to find a small slow cooker that will suit your needs. If you are going to look into a professional hot stone heater on Amazon or massage products stores, you should know that many of them give off an unpleasant odor. Read the reviews carefully before settling on your chosen heater.

Beverages and Snacks

A nice touch for any massage therapy practice is the provision of complimentary beverages. In the winter, your customers will get a kick out of an offer of warm apple cider, hot tea or chocolate.

If you want to offer two or more packages for special promotions, like ½ day packages for Mother's Day, give your customer a small break in between sessions with a complimentary beverage and snack. You can buy individualized size packages of nuts, candies or crackers. Fresh fruit is always a crowd pleaser.

Presentation, though, is of paramount importance. It just feels more self-indulgent when you can recline in a soft robe and enjoy a refreshing beverage or snack. It's that feeling of king or queen for a day that will keep your customers coming back for more. Serve their cold water or fruit juice in a nice glass.

Cocktail glasses often look appealing, filled with a refreshing beverage.

You may also want to consider to-go cups for clients to take a beverage with them, especially in the winter months. Imagine receiving a wonderful massage then be given a complimentary cup of hot chocolate or warm tea on your way out the door. Fill of coffee maker with only hot water, then offer a selection of beverage choices. This extra will leave a lasting impression.

These are the little things that make a big difference to your bottom line. Smart marketer's get repeat customers by going the extra mile on the little things.

Different Types of Packages

Packages for Face and Scalp:

Kansa Contouring Face Massage

Hot Stone Face Massage

Asian Spoon Face Massage

Hot Oil Scalp Massage

Hydrating Face Mask

Aromatherapy Face and Scalp Massage

Packages for Feet and Hands:

Hydrating Hand and Foot

Shea Butter Treatments & Scents

Peppermint Foot Mask

Hot Stone Hand and Foot Massage

Sugar Scrubs

Foot Soaks

Paraffin Wax Hand and Foot Treatments

Full Body Packages:

Scented Hydrating Body Treatment

Vitamin Rich Body Treatment (with exfoliation)

Dry Brushing (dry brush gloves are easy to use and easy to clean)

Seasonal Body Treatments - seasonal scents

Stress Buster Detoxifying Body

Wrap Bamboo Massage

Gentleman Massage Package

Sports Massage

Corestone Massage

Himalayan Salt Stones

Specialty Packages or Add Ons Cupping

Raindrop Therapy

Cranial Sacral Lymphatic

Energy Work

  Matrix Energetics – Two Point

  Access Conscious – Run Bars

Reiki

Western & Eastern Massage

Mixture Trigger Point

Shiatsu Thai Pregnancy

Yoga Massage

Special Occasion Packages

Mother's Day - Father's Day

Sweethearts - Valentine's

Birthday Celebration

Anniversary

Any holiday – St Patrick's Day, Earth Day

Bridal Showers

Packages Names and Descriptions

Sample packages can be used word for word. You can also pull out your favorite descriptions or slogans and create your own packages. Create a menu with different price points and length of services.

During holiday season you will sell an abundance of gift cards. One selling strategy is to offer 2 or 3 packages with different price ranges. We see siblings chipping in together to treat their parents to couples packages. New relationships often buy their partner the gift of massage. The variety of packages allows all individuals, regardless of their budget, to give the gift of relaxation.

Have gift bags displayed for attractive gift card sale presentation. Candy inside the gift bag is appealing and gives more value to the package.

Zen Package

50-minute package includes relaxing face massage with hot stones and hydrating pomegranate face lotion. Facial pressure points help release sinus. Great for anyone with TMJ issues.

Package includes hot oil scalp massage. Hot moisturizing oils of jojoba, grapeseed, sesame, apricot and aloe vera are used to massage the scalp. Try the hot oil scalp massage for that fabulous feel that helps with dry skin or hair loss.

Kansa Facial & Foot Treatment

Facial treatment with Kansa wand. Tightens and tones skin, moves lymph and opens sinuses. Kansa face massage uses a handheld contoured tool to balance the Ayurvedic doshes.

Package includes foot massage with Kansa wand for whole-body balancing.

Bamboo Melt Away

Melt away pain and stress with a warm 75-minute bamboo massage. Package starts with dry brush massage to move lymph and exfoliate dead skin cells. Bamboo massage is a relaxing therapeutic massage that helps loosen the most stubborn knots and muscles. The warmth of the bamboo as well as long soothing techniques help diminish spasms and relieve stress. Pain and tension just fade away.

Celebration Package

Start your experience on a warm heated massage table. Package includes an aromatherapy scalp massage and hot stone back massage. De-stress during the calming 50 minute package.

Bamboo / Hot Stone Fusion Package

Experience the best of Eastern massage. Warm bamboo massage paired with hot stones. This combination massage package is a customer favorite! This therapeutic package releases sore and aching muscles while you feel drift into a place of peace and serenity.

Hawaiian Escape

Enjoy an escape to Hawaii. Start your Polynesian journey with a hydrating jasmine face massage. Your getaway includes a soothing Hawaiian Lomi Lomi massage with moisturizing tropical scents. One hour of uninterrupted me time to decompress and rejuvenate the body, mind and spirit.

Himalayan Salt Stone Massage

This healing massage uses heated Himalayan salt stones to reduce tension and relieve pain and inflammation. Through osmosis, the salt's minerals and nutrients naturally activate your healing mechanisms, allowing your body to restore itself to balance.

Chakra Balancing

Chakras are energy centers that affect our immune and endocrine systems. Negative information can adversely affect the body and spirit; this energy-balancing treatment uses gemstones to help clear the chakras, calm the mind and improve your body's ability to self heal.

Lavender Infusion Package

60-minute session with calm, soothing lavender scalp massage. Full body massage that includes hot stones on back. Hydrating lavender butter hand and foot treatment.

Bali Bliss Indulgence

Enjoy this ultimate 90-minute package of bliss. Select your favorite scent for your calming scalp massage. The package includes deep relaxing hot stones on back and feet. A mango sugar foot scrub sure to revitalize and balance your body.

Balanced Soles

Step into complete balance with a reflexology and acupressure foot package. Enjoy a peppermint foot masque followed by a hot towel foot treatment and hot stone foot massage.

Couples Massage Packages

Our couples signature massages include aromatherapy scalp massage. Pick your scent: *peppermint *lavender *orange *lemon *eucalyptus.

Hold hands as you de-stress together. Massage includes deep relaxing hot stones and hot towels. Massage releases feel good hormones and increases happiness. Couples who massage together, stay together!

Additional package names:

Relaxation Package

Tranquility Package

Serenity Package

Joy Package

Peace Package

Ultimate Package

(your business name) Signature Package

Mix and Match Package

Pick your favorites and customize the perfect massage for you! (have list of your therapy enhancements)

60 minutes - pick 2 therapy enhancements 90 minutes - pick 3 therapy enhancements

Express Massage

If you have limited time, enjoy one of our express massage for singles or couples. 30 or 45 minute massage focusing on one or two muscle groups of their choice.

(Basic express couples massage is very popular. It is an affordable date idea. The express package allows people to try massage at lower price. Instead of advertising it as a budget massage, express massage is a nice way to offer a basic short session. The most common response is, they fall in love with massage and return for longer sessions with upgrades.)

1/2 Day Package

Celebrate you with half day of pampering services. Pick any 2 of our treatments (have list of 50 or 60 minute packages). In between your treatments enjoy a light snack and beverage.

2 1/2 hours of Bliss!

Full Day Package

Indulge is a day of luxury. You can allow customer to pick the treatments or you can have specific treatments. Include light lunch. You can allow them to pick from some menu options. For example, if you are going to bring in Subway, you can have them select their lunch choice at time of booking.

Don't Leave that Money on the Table!

As a massage therapist, you genuinely want to deliver the best for your clients. It is criminally negligent not to expect the same for yourself.

This book has given you many ideas that are guaranteed to help you transform your business fortunes. You can't be at your best for your clients if you aren't deriving satisfaction from your practice, both professional and financial.

The principles you've read in this book are the culmination of my many years of trial and error and struggle and success in the massage therapy industry. I am glad that you not only purchased this book, but took the time to read it through. This demonstrates a commitment on your part to take charge of your business future. All that is left is to take these ideas, get out there and put them into practice and watch your massage therapy practice flourish!

Jumpstart your business by hiring your own business consultant. Sabrina has a special offer for you found on her website. http://www.massagemarketing101.com/consultant

www.ingramcontent.com/pod-product-compliance
Lightning Source LLC
Chambersburg PA
CBHW071457070426
42452CB00040B/1860